by DeeAnn Moshier

as compiled by Dr. Randy T. Johnson

COVER DESIGNER
Dani Reynolds

INTERIOR DESIGNER
Shawna Johnson

First Edition, July 2016

Published by:
The River Church
8393 E. Holly Rd.
Holly, MI 48442

Scriptures are taken from the Bible,
English Standard Version (ESV)

THE RIVER CHURCH

Printed in the United States of America

CONTENTS

Why NOT Me?

Cancer. That word should not start a sentence, paragraph, chapter, or even a book. For many, it has been viewed as a "death sentence." For one lady, she acknowledged that it brought her to a point focusing on a venture in meaningful life for her and others.

Dee started this series saying, "Lord willing these will be the lessons we will discuss." She then shared the topics. The lessons were designed to show what she was learning from her battle with cancer. The victory of remission was short lived. She entered the new stages from the trenches bearing her heart to ladies every Monday night.

The series started in September of 2015. She entered the presence of the Lord in June of 2016, but her lessons will continue in the lives of the many people she touched.

PREFACE

Pastor Jim Combs

God gave me the privilege of serving Jesus with Dee Moshier for over 30 years. She was born ten days before me in the same town. We went to school together as kids. I remember when she first met her husband Rich and how she immediately announced she was going to marry him. Carole and I have five children, and we always appreciated "Miss Dee" helping out.

I was thinking about Dee's life, and God brought a specific passage to my mind. Luke 10:38-42 says, "Now as they went on their way, Jesus entered a village. And a woman named Martha welcomed him into her house. And she had a sister called Mary, who sat at the Lord's feet and listened to his teaching. But Martha was distracted with much serving. And she went up to him and said, 'Lord, do you not care that my sister has left me to serve alone? Tell her then to help me.' But the Lord answered her, 'Martha, Martha, you are anxious and troubled about many things, but one thing is necessary. Mary has chosen the good portion, which will not be taken away from her.'"

There were these two amazing ladies who honestly both loved Jesus. The first was Martha. She was the one who greeted

Jesus at the door, made dinner, was running back and forth, organizing, structuring, and putting everything in order. Dee too was organized. She had her beloved Franklin Planner. It covered everything from what she was cooking for dinner each day to what she would wear. I have never met a greater Martha in my entire life. She served Jesus with a passion. The last text she sent me said, "Nobody understands what it means to do what we do because it isn't work for us. It is who we are." She loved serving Jesus. While serving our church, she helped at least two other local churches get their books in order, one in another state, and even a Christian camp. She had the Martha part down.

Dee wasn't satisfied with being a Martha. The conversation Jesus has with these two ladies is interesting. He basically tells Martha she is doing amazing stuff, but she doesn't get it. He acknowledged that she was working hard and serving people. It was good. However, good wasn't enough. He goes on to say that Mary has chosen the better things. Mary chose to sit at the feet of Jesus.

These last few years I have had the privilege of watching Dee grow into one of the godliest women I have ever known. She chose to sit at the feet of Jesus. As life got tougher, she started taking on the characteristics of Mary. She just wanted to be in His presence and feel His presence every day. She learned how to take people to the feet of Jesus and explain what it looks like. Dee was a godly woman.

I am so thankful and blessed for having had the great privilege of serving alongside an incredible Martha and an amazing Mary.

I encourage you to read Dee's lessons and better learn how to be the hands and feet of Jesus while creating time to sit at His feet.

1

SUBMISSION

J eremiah 29:11 - *"For I know the plans I have for you, declares the Lord, plans for welfare and not for evil, to give you a future and a hope."*

Submission is defined as the state of being obedient: the act of accepting the authority or control of someone else. Last January God put me on a path that I would never have chosen on my own but that taught me the value of true submission.

Do people struggle with being submissive? Why or Why not?

_____

_____

_____

Do you struggle with being submissive? Why or Why not?

_____

_____

_____

The captain of the ship looked into the dark night and saw faint lights in the distance. Immediately he told his signalman to send a message: "Alter your course 10 degrees south." Promptly a return message was received: "Alter your course 10 degrees north."

The captain was angered; his command had been ignored. So he sent a second message: "Alter your course 10 degrees south. I am the captain!" Soon another message was received: "Alter your course 10 degrees north. I am seaman third class Bruder." Immediately the captain sent a third message, knowing the fear it would evoke: "Alter your course 10 degrees south. I am a battleship." Then the reply came: "Alter your course 10 degrees north. I am a lighthouse."

I think it is fair to say that most men struggle with pride and therefore submission. We know about that male ego.

Let's talk about children and their selective hearing.

Can you think of a story of a child that was resisting authority (maybe the question should be – can you think of a child that did not resist authority)? _____

_____

_____

I remember the story of a child refusing to sit down. Finally, his mom physically sat him down. He said, "I may be sitting down on the outside, but I am standing on the inside."

How often do you act that way? _____

_____

_____

(We may not be kicking our feet outwardly, but we are kicking and screaming against God inside.)

Why do you say no to candy, insist on healthy food, and regular bedtimes for your children? _____

_____

_____

Luke 11:13 says, *"If you then, who are evil, know how to give good gifts to your children, how much more will the heavenly Father give the Holy Spirit to those who ask him!"*

If you expect your children to "submit" and trust you, why don't you trust your heavenly Father? _____

_____

_____

Children are needy. They do not always know what is best for them. We know what is best for our children. They need to submit to us.

We are needy. We do not always know what is best for us. God knows what is best for His children. We need to submit to Him.

Name some examples of your New Year's resolutions.

_____

_____

_____

How many have you kept? _____

_____

_____

I keep very few. A couple years ago, I decided instead of making a New Year's Resolution, I would ask God something He wants me to be working on for the year to be able to serve Him better.

That January he laid on my heart "Be submissive." I thought, "That's a great idea, Lord, because my husband Rich is going to retire soon. As you (God) know, I run everything. I run our social calendar, our money, and his honey-do list. Since I hope to work for another 20-30 years (my mom is 76 and still works 4 days a week) it will be good for me to allow my husband to be in charge of these things." Actually, I have taught on this to women, but I have not put it in practice much. I knew God said in Ephesians 5:22, *"Wives, submit to your own husbands, as to the Lord."* Now it was time for me to take a step in spiritual maturity and submit to the Lord.

Side note: God has to tell us to submit because we, as women, naturally (in the flesh) struggle in this area. Even back to Eve, and with no peer pressure or TV to influence her, she did not like being told there was one tree she could not eat of.

The Bible also teaches submission to others. The verse right before the command for women to submit says, *"Submitting to one another out of reverence for Christ"* (Ephesians 5:21). Submission needs to be part of everyone's walk.

It is safe to say that men, children, women, and therefore everyone have to work at being submissive.

There is an old covered wooden bridge "up north" (northern part of Michigan). It is narrow, as it was not designed for cars, but walking and carriages. As you enter the bridge from the south, there is a yield sign. Once you know it is clear, you enter through.

Interesting enough, there is a yield sign on the other side too. Learning to yield in life helps us avoid interpersonal head-on collisions.

Job 22:21 says, *"Agree with God, and be at peace; thereby good will come to you."* The word agree can be translated submit. We need to focus more on agreeing in the Lord and with the Lord as part of our transformation in to being submissive.

Why should you want to learn to be submissive?

_____

_____

_____

Philippians 4:7 answers, *"And the peace of God, which surpasses all understanding, will guard your hearts and your minds in Christ Jesus."*

Why would you want to have peace? _____

_____

_____

The Greek word "guard" is "phroureō" which means to prevent hostile invasion. If we have the "peace of God", it will guard our hearts (feelings) and mind (thoughts) from hostile invasion (Satan and his demons).

What image comes to mind when you think of "hostile invasion?"

_____

_____

_____

So, last January I began my journey in submission. Little did I know He had much greater plans in this area than just submitting to my husband.

In February 2014, our church hired John to be our Financial Director. You need to realize, I have been in charge of the finances here for 24 of the 30 years I have worked here. Now we are hiring someone to do MY job! Then I remembered – Aha! – God wants me to be submissive to this change. I can do this. I met with John when we hired him and explained my challenge from God and told him my goal was to be as much of a help to him as I could. I must say it has been an awesome transition. If I had let my heart and mind be invaded by the enemy and got an attitude, it would have been so much more difficult on me and on the ministry of our church.

In early spring, I began to feel "unwell." I had heartburn and stomach aches a lot. I did a food diary and determined I had become allergic to dairy. This was my diagnosis because I do not go to doctors.

August came, and I was still nauseous and fatigued. My husband began asking me to go to the doctor, but I am never sick, and those are vague symptoms. So I put him off, and we planned our summer vacation. I was very sick our whole vacation and did not have the energy to participate in many activities. I did have three grandchildren with me so I attributed it to this.

Before you know it, it was the week after Labor Day. In my job at church, every fall is our "fresh start." Job definitions are redefined, and changes are made (but never to me). Pastor Jim (the Lead Pastor) calls me in his office to "have a talk" (this is usually what happens to others – LOL). He proceeds to tell me what a good employee I am and blah, blah, blah, but.... He needs a male assistant so he can travel with him and attend functions with him, so Noble would now be his Administrative Assistant.

Of course, everybody else (staff, friends, and family) is all worried about my feelings, but I have been preparing to be submissive and acceptable of change. This must be the final submissive thing God is going to have in my life – right? I mean, this is a big one. Where do I fit on our staff now? John is doing the finances and Noble is Pastor Jim's assistant, both my previous job descriptions. However, I have peace about these changes, because I have been practicing "submission." I need to remind you that this is not easy, and my flesh wants its own way (selfishness), but I am working hard at this peace I desire and pleasing my Lord.

The following Monday I was exceptionally sick and my husband insisted I go to my family doctor. It "just so happens" he had an appointment available at 2:00 pm on that same day, so I left to do the church banking and then over to the doctor. Of course, my symptoms are vague, but he assumes gallbladder. I am now lying on the table so he can feel my stomach and he finds a "mass." I can tell by his face that it is not a good thing. He says, "I think you need an x-ray." I go have an x-ray done and when the results come in he says, "Well, you have a 15 x 14 x 16 cm mass. I want you to have CT scan. Probably just a fibroid but let's check it out." That weekend I attended a Beth Moore Simulcast in Illinois with my girls and friends, so I put the scan off until the following week. I am a little worried, but since nothing usually happens to me, I figure the worse is I have to have surgery. Of course, I start "planning" the right time to have this minor surgery like when can I fit it in my schedule with all the things I already have planned to do.

After the results of my CT scan had come back as metastasized ovarian cancer, I began to realize I had a long journey in front of me that God had been preparing me for. HE just needs me to be submissive to HIS plans and HE will "direct my path." I made an appointment with the oncologist who my daughter-in-law (a nurse at St. Joe's) recommended. He usually cannot see people for months but it "just so happens" I could get in the next day.

While my husband and I were in his office, he read my CT scan report and said he thought sounded to him as if it was just a benign ovarian cyst. There only is a 9% chance it is cancer, so, for the most part, I was not worried, and they scheduled surgery the next Friday, September 26.

That day we are supposed to go on a long weekend that been "planned" for ages. I ask if we can delay my surgery to I can keep my plans, and the doctor said, "NO," and again a little thought popped into my head that it is more serious than I think.

Early in the morning of September 26, my husband and I head to St. Joseph Mercy Hospital for my surgery and quick recovery. When I woke up in the evening (several hours later), I see my family and Pastor Jim standing around me, just looking. I thought, "This is not a good thing." Pastor Jim leans down by my side and tells me I have cancer. Of course, he did not tell me how extensive. He just said, "We are going to fight and win this battle."

After a while in recovery, my blood pressure and heart rate would not stabilize and after many doctors and tests, I was sent to ICU. I now realize this is not going to be a quick recovery. I was there for three days and another two days on the surgical floor. I had a 13-inch incision, and they had removed the tumor (which was benign), my appendix, ovaries, omentum, and removed cancer from various other places but did leave cancer on my colon to prevent a colostomy bag (which I am grateful for).

So the question is WHY ME?

The answer is WHY NOT ME!

As I turn to the Word, these verses come to mind.

John 9:1-3 helps me relate to what God might have for me: *"As he passed by, he saw a man blind from birth. And his disciples asked him, 'Rabbi, who sinned, this man or his parents, that he was born blind?' Jesus answered, 'It was not that this man sinned, or his parents, but that the works of God might be displayed in him.'"*

Why was the man born blind? _____
_____
_____

God allows difficulties for at least three reasons (this is part of the answer to why God allows bad things to happen to good people). First, struggles can come as a result of our own poor and even sinful choices. This could be seen in financial struggles through overuse of a credit card. Second, being knocked down may be the only way we learn to look up. Our trial may draw us to Him. Third, my pain may be so that others are drawn to God. This is where the works of God are displayed through us.

A man was blind for 38 years. His blindness very well may have been the only way he would "see" Jesus as Lord and Savior. His blindness allowed others to "see" the power of God. Clearly, it was worth it.

My prayer was and is that the works of God might be displayed through me and that I will gain endurance, character, and hope so that I will not shame my Lord and that I might be perfect and complete, lacking nothing.

Do you desire that the works of God be displayed through you?

_____

_____

_____

Romans 5:3-5 says, *"Not only that, but we rejoice in our sufferings, knowing that suffering produces endurance, and endurance produces character, and character produces hope, and hope does not put us to shame, because God's love has been poured into our hearts through the Holy Spirit who has been given to us."*

How is it possible to "rejoice in your sufferings?"

_____

_____

_____

James 1:2-4 says, *"Count it all joy, my brothers, when you meet trials of various kinds, for you know that the testing of your faith produces steadfastness. And let steadfastness have its full effect, that you may be perfect and complete, lacking in nothing."*

Why do you struggle with control? _____

_____

_____

Is there anything you would want more than *"that you may be perfect and complete, lacking in nothing?"* _____

_____

_____

_____

What does that verse mean? _____

_____

_____

If we believe God is in control, and we trust that He loves us and only wants to do the best for us, then we will submit our will. (Remember our definition-the act of accepting the authority or control of someone else.)

God has blessed me tremendously with healing. I am taking my family away on the anniversary date of my diagnosis last year and for the length of time I was in the hospital. I want to celebrate God's goodness to us as a family and make new memories for this time.

The goal of this study is to share my process and willingness (sometimes forced) to submit to His plan and discuss how these principles can apply to our lives.

My prayer for you is that through these lessons you will be thankful for all He does for you and will let His peace rule in your heart and guard your feelings and thoughts by living life in His plans.

The chorus to "Oceans"
(My favorite song before I was diagnosed):

Spirit lead me where my trust is without borders
Let me walk upon the waters
Wherever You would call me
Take me deeper than my feet could ever wander
And my faith will be made stronger
In the presence of my Savior

2

FRANKLIN PLANNER

J eremiah 29:11 - *"For I know the plans I have for you, declares the Lord, plans for welfare and not for evil, to give you a future and a hope."*

How effective are you in starting each day looking for God's plan not your own plan? Evaluating our prayers might help decipher this. _____

_____

_____

I have been diagnosed with OCD (it should be CDO so it would be in alphabetical order) and mine most often shows itself in the need to organize and plan. I have a Franklin Planner, and I would drive people crazy trying to make them "commit" to my plans so I can plan more things. The more things I plan, the more I need to plan. I also drive my husband crazy with my need to organize. One that is quite extreme is that I alphabetize my clothes (at least that doesn't affect other people). My clothes are "filed" in my closet by color and then listed in an excel sheet.

When the results of my CT scan came back with probable metastasized ovarian cancer, I began to realize I had a long journey in front of me that God had been preparing me for. However, I am still trying to fit it in my Franklin Planner. After I had met with Dr. Hicks, my oncologist, and he said I would need surgery I started "planning" the right time to have this "minor" surgery. When can I fit surgery in my schedule with all the things I already had planned to do?

Being a prepared employee, I did meet with Pastor Jim to tell him "my plan" for work. I prepared payroll and bills for the week following my surgery and then I would come back the following week for 3 days, and then after that, I would be back to normal.

Dr. Hicks met with me on day four after my surgery and explained that I would be doing six months of chemo. The side effects were that I would lose my hair (I had four future hair appointments already planned in my Franklin planner), I would be nauseous, fatigued, and numerous other side effects. This was not in my plans!

During the summer, before I was diagnosed I had begun writing a lesson on "The Best Laid Plans of Mice and Men Often Go Awry." This saying is from a poem written by Robert Burns in 1785 to a mouse. According to legend, Burns wrote the poem after finding a nest full of mice during the winter. It tells of how he, while plowing a field, upturned a mouse's nest. The resulting poem is an apology to the mouse:
>"But, Mousie, you aren't alone
>In proving foresight may be vain:
>The best laid schemes o' mice an' men often go awry
>And leave us nothing but grief and pain,
>Instead of promised joy."

Before cancer (I call this BC), even the slightest shift from my plan in my Franklin would cause me tension and often unchristian-like reactions to people. All the planning did not bring me peace but instead added stress to my life. It was difficult to try to achieve and keep "my plans." I kept making checklists of what I needed to do to gain control of my life and the harder I tried, the more frustrated I become.

I wish I could just relax and be at peace.

After cancer (referred to as AC), God showed me this verse:

Jeremiah 29:11 - ***"For I know the plans I have for you, declares the Lord, plans for welfare and not for evil, to give you a future and a hope."***

As I pondered this, I realized that all my planning was in vain. God's plan usurped my plans whether I allowed it or not. The only thing I had control over was in my willingness to submit (remember this definition from previous lesson - the state of being obedient; the act of accepting the authority or control of someone else).

I gave up making any plans for a while, but God made me the way He made me, and I like to plan. There is nothing wrong with planning things (and I still think it helps to accomplish more). I like to say, "A lack of planning on your part should not create an emergency on my part." We need to remember, "God knows the plans He has for us, for peace and not for evil (or to harm us)."

My new motto is…
Make your plans in pencil and let God put them in ink.

An acronym for PLAN has helped me.

P is for pray.

How should we do this?

Proverbs 16:3 says, *"Commit your work to the Lord, and your plans will be established."*

How can you commit your work to God?

To start with, we need to give Him each day by spending time with Him.

How do you tend to start your day? _____
_____
_____

I started mine by giving God a copy of my itinerary and appointment schedule and praying for His blessing on it.

Maybe we should begin with asking God to guide and direct our day and its plans.

Our prayer should be:
"Dear God, you have so many plans prepared for me. Things YOU want me to say and do that will show others your power, provision, protection, and promises. I pray that I will not let my own goals and dreams stand in the way of you using me. I can be stubborn and want what I want, but in the end, I know your plans will be

established with or without me and I don't want to miss out on seeing you work in and through my life. Amen." (From Focus of Hope Facebook page – Tonia Harrison)

The L in PLAN is for Live. Live for today.

Is there anything from your past holding you back?

_____

_____

_____

Do you struggle more with living off past victories or feeling defeated due to past failures? _____

_____

_____

Strive to live for today. We cannot change the past. God is offering a fresh start.

Proverbs 27:1 says, ***"Do not boast about tomorrow, for you do not know what a day may bring."***

James 4:13-14 continues the thought, ***"Come now, you who say, 'Today or tomorrow we will go into such and such a town and spend a year there and trade and make a profit' - yet you do not know what tomorrow will bring. What is your life? For you are a mist that appears for a little time and then vanishes."***

We need to give God our present day. When we speak of the future with unearned confidence, we are talking in pride. We end up pushing God aside, grabbing the reins, and taking full control. We need to remember that tomorrow is not promised to us.

There is a belief called the "arrival fallacy." It states, "When you arrive you will be happy," but the fallacy is though you may anticipate great happiness in arrival, arriving rarely makes you as happy as you anticipated.

When I have money, when I get married, when the kids are grown, when I finish school... We need to seek, follow, and please God today.

There is also something known as the grass is greener syndrome. We keep waiting for the grass to be greener to enjoy our life. If we work on enjoying the present, we do not need to count on happiness in the future. There may not be a future - here.

What are you waiting on "someday" for? _____

_____

_____

What memory of enjoyment do you have from the past?

_____

_____

_____

Psalm 118:24 says, *This is the day that the Lord has made; let us rejoice and be glad in it.*

How does this verse relate to our past? Our future?

_____

_____

_____

The A in PLAN is for Accomplish. We need to accomplish His purpose.

Proverbs 19:21 adds, *"Many are the plans in the mind of a man, but it is the purpose of the Lord that will stand."*

Can you think back over your life and recall what kind of plans you had for your life in your teens? _____
_____
_____

Your twenties? _____
_____
_____

Your thirties? _____
_____
_____

How many of those seem foolish years later?
_____
_____
_____

If it eventually is the purpose of the Lord that will stand, then why do we think we need to take control?
_____
_____
_____

It is not wrong to have plans, but when we commit all our time and energy into pursuing what we want and not taking God's plans into consideration, they become an unhealthy obsession.

Do you go to sleep at night with a list of what you did not accomplish and wake in the morning with a list of what is waiting for you? _____

_____

_____

What does God want you to accomplish that you are putting off because of your own plans? _____

_____

_____

His purpose will stand, and He will accomplish His plans with or without you.

King Solomon recounts his life spent pursuing after what he wanted: ***"But as I looked at everything I had worked so hard to accomplish, it was all so meaningless; like chasing the wind. There was nothing really worthwhile anywhere"*** (Ecclesiastes 2:11 NLT).

Why not let it be you God uses to fulfill His plans. Do not miss the blessings that come from being the one God works in and through. Do not spend your life chasing after the wind.

The N in PLAN is for Notice. In difficult times it's easy to overlook our relationship with God. Our focus should not be on the plan but to take notice of God and strive to know Him.

Most important thing: Do you know God? _____

_____

_____

How can you know God or know Him better? _____

_____

_____

Only with a personal relationship with God, through our Lord and Savior Jesus Christ, can God's plan and guidance be a part of your life.

I thought, "If only I could figure out God's plan, then I would be all set." I Googled "God's plan" and thousands of results came up. Many of the ideas were about focusing, finding, and following God's plan for me (and you, too).

However, God is not going to tell us the plan. God's plan is on a need-to-know basis, and apparently, He thinks we do not need to know.

When you tell your kids to get in the car, do you tell them where you are going every time?

Do they ask? _____

_____

_____

Often they just do what they are told. Why? _____

_____

_____

They do what they are told because they "know" you. They "know" you are not taking them anywhere that is bad for them. They "know" they can trust you enough to get in the car even if they do not know where they are going.

The problem is most of us adults do not have that kind of trust with God. If Jesus Himself drove up to our house and said, "Get in," we would have some questions we would want answered. "Where are we going?" "How long is this going to take?" "What do I need?" "Will it hurt?" "Why do we have to go there?"

What question do you think you would ask?

_____

_____

_____

We would waste a bunch of time trying to figure out what Jesus had planned before we agreed to go along. That is how most of us live our lives. We are obsessed with finding things out, especially as they relate to our lives and us. We want to know where we are headed, how we are getting there, how long it will take, what will we need, will it hurt, and why?

We will not budge until we have all those questions answered.

When we look backward, we can see God's plan being worked out. Often it has turned out different (but better, or at least more interesting than we could have planned.) It takes a lot of time and perspective to be able to see God's plans at work. We often cannot see God in the moment. God does not tell us the future. Sometimes we get little glimpses of where we are going, but most of the time it is a matter of trust.

We need to "Know" God, not the Plan.

The secret to finding out God's plan for your life is not to keep asking God to tell you the plan. It is trusting Him for the ride. It does not matter where God is taking you. Just go.

The reality is none of us knows where God is taking us and our obsession with knowing the plan is just our obsession with control. We want to know so we can feel more in control of our destiny. God has never promised to tell us the plan for our lives. He has only promised that if we want to, we can know Him.

From Sarah Young's devotion "Jesus Calling" on September 17:
You will not find my (God's) peace by engaging in excessive planning, attempting to control what will happen to you in the future. That is a commonly practiced form of unbelief. When your mind spins with multiple plans, peace may sometimes be within your grasp, yet it always eludes you.

Proverbs 16:9 says, ***"The heart of man plans his way, but the Lord establishes his steps."***

Isaiah 26:3 says, ***"You keep him in perfect peace whose mind is stayed on you, because he trusts in you."***

How do these verses challenge or encourage you?

_____

_____

_____

Remember to PLAN:

Pray

Live for today

Accomplish His purpose

Notice God

3

BITTER OR BETTER

J eremiah 29:11 - *"For I know the plans I have for you, declares the Lord, plans for welfare and not for evil, to give you a future and a hope."*

"One's philosophy is not best expressed in words; it is expressed in the choices one makes... and the choices we make are ultimately our responsibility."   Eleanor Roosevelt

Luke 15:11-32
"And he said, 'There was a man who had two sons. And the younger of them said to his father, 'Father, give me the share of property that is coming to me.' And he divided his property between them. Not many days later, the younger son gathered all he had and took a journey into a far country, and there he squandered his property in reckless living. And when he had spent everything, a severe famine arose in that country, and he began to be in need. So he went and hired himself out to one of the citizens of that country, who sent him into his fields to feed pigs. And he was longing to be fed with the pods that the pigs ate, and no one gave him anything.

But when he came to himself, he said, 'How many of my father's hired servants have more than enough bread, but I perish here with hunger! I will arise and go to my father, and I will say to him, 'Father, I have sinned against heaven and before you. I am no longer worthy to be called your son. Treat me as one of your hired servants.' And he arose and came to his father. But while he was still a long way off, his father saw him and felt compassion, and ran and embraced him and kissed him. And the son said to him, 'Father, I have sinned against heaven and before you. I am no longer worthy to be called your son.' But the father said to his servants, 'Bring quickly the best robe, and put it on him, and put a ring on his hand, and shoes on his feet. And bring the fattened calf and kill it, and let us eat and celebrate. For this my son was dead, and is alive again; he was lost, and is found.' And they began to celebrate.

Now his older son was in the field, and as he came and drew near to the house, he heard music and dancing. And he called one of the servants and asked what these things meant. And he said to him, 'Your brother has come, and your father has killed the fattened calf, because he has received him back safe and sound.' But he was angry and refused to go in. His father came out and entreated him, but he answered his father, 'Look, these many years I have served you, and I never disobeyed your command, yet you never gave me a young goat, that I might celebrate with my friends. But when this son of yours came, who has devoured your property with prostitutes, you killed the fattened calf for him!' And he said to him, 'Son, you are always with me, and all that is mine is yours. It was fitting to celebrate and be glad, for this your brother was dead, and is alive; he was lost, and is found.'"

"Every time I see my brother, I just praise God for God's grace in his life. Because if God can change Franklin from a prodigal into a man of God, he can do it for anybody." Anne Graham Lotz

Most people are familiar with this story and focus on the father and the prodigal son; however, there are three lessons we can learn from the older brother:

1. We can choose God's plan or choose to miss the party.

"But he was angry and refused to go in."

Why do you think the older brother refused to go in?

_____

_____

_____

Maybe the older brother is on a program of self-salvation, earning the approval of his community and the favor of his father. However, when he feels the terms of this deal are violated, his good attitude evaporates into resentment.

I played by the rules and believed my good behavior was an attempt to earn God's approval and maybe even obligate Him to do what I want.

Maybe the father in Jesus' story felt he could honor and bless his oldest boy MORE by inviting him into the deep relationship of mutual service than by merely giving him a party of his own.

Maybe becoming a Christian is not only accepting Jesus into my life, but also accepting His incredible invitation to be a part of His life. Having a party thrown in one's honor is a blessing, but being invited to help him throw the party is a vastly greater gift. The Father is hosting a lavish banquet, and we are invited, not because "we followed the rules," but because He loves us.

I have always participated in ministry, but now I love doing ministry and appreciate the opportunity to speak, serve, and try to be a blessing. As a result of choosing to accept God's plan, I get to be a real part of God's ministry serving through and with Him while enjoying the party!

What ministry(s) are you missing out in by refusing to accept God's Plans? _____

_____

_____

2. Even if we do not choose His plan, God still loves us.

"His father came out and entreated him."

Entreat: call to or call upon, which may be done in the way of exhortation, comfort, or instruction, to ask a person earnestly; beseech; implore; beg, to make a request or petition.

The attitude of the father toward the older brother is the same as the attitude toward the younger brother. The father left the feast to seek out his elder son rather than waiting for the elder son to come to him. The father offered love and grace to both sons, and with the same paternal compassion with which he had fallen on the neck of the younger, he comes and pleads with the elder. His loving compassion entreats him to change his attitude and join in the party.

Just as the father left the party to meet his older son, with mercy and grace our God in Christ, will leave the party. In His tender and gentle ways, He still leaves the banquet table, the dancing and the partying, and meets us, where we are, with that same gentle invitation. "Come to the feast. Come to the banquet. Don't you know, everything I have, including my LOVE, has always been there for you?"

Is there a time you doubted God's love for you?

_____

_____

_____

Who do we hurt by being bitter, by not going to the party?

_____

_____

_____

3. Instead of accepting God's plans, you might get bitter.

"But he answered his father, 'Look, these many years I have served you, and I never disobeyed your command, yet you never gave me a young goat, that I might celebrate with my friends.'"

The older brother says, *"I have never disobeyed your commands."*

This kind of exaggeration is normal for those who harbor bitterness in their heart. Never and always are common words. The proud and the self-righteous always feel that they are not treated as well as they deserve.

They (we) grumble - they got what I didn't

They (we) pout - why did bad things happen to me?

They (we) boast - I followed rules and played fairly, better than anyone else.

They (we) whine - nobody cares about me.

Have you ever felt like you were not treated as you deserved?

_____

_____

_____

Certainly, this younger brother had been a prisoner - a prisoner of sin, stupidity, and a pigsty. The older brother lives in some confinement, too. He has, as yet, been unable to break out of the prison of himself. He feels taken for granted by his father and alienated by his brother when neither is the case.

Who is it that whispers so subtly in our ear that a gift given to another somehow diminishes the blessings we have received? Who makes us feel that if God is smiling on another, then He surely must somehow be frowning on us? Who makes us feel when bad things happen that God does not love us anymore or He left us?

_____

_____

_____

You and I both know who does this—it is the father of all lies.

When you focus on what you do not have or on a situation that displeases you, your mind becomes darkened. In addition, when we criticize or complain we are acting as if we could run the world better than God could.

If you could change the world, what would you do different?

_____

_____

_____

Would you remove freewill and its consequences? Should love be forced or chosen? _____

_____

_____

Read John 16:33 (*"I have said these things to you, that in me you may have peace. In the world you will have tribulation. But take heart; I have overcome the world."*) What does Jesus tell you? _____

_____

_____

Jesus tells us – we will have trouble in this world. We will suffer; we will endure heartache and hardship.

What does Luke 15:31 say? I love the answer that the father gives to the prodigal son's older, more faithful brother:

"And he said to him, 'Son, you are always with me, and all that is mine is yours."

Each moment you can choose to practice His presence or to practice the presence of your problems.

What does our Father give us? <u>A relationship with Him</u>

What else did the older brother have?

He had his job, his health, his home, respect of his father, his inheritance, his good name...

So, instead of focusing on what I had in Jesus, I was focusing on what I didn't have and wanted. This can cause you to be angry (bitter) at others who got what you did not. It is not fair. But really, who else deserves this diagnosis? This way of thinking keeps you in bondage.

Sometimes you have to look for the good. It is a choice that you have to make to be submissive to His plan.

We will never know if the elder brother listened to the wise counsel of his father.

What would be the results of his life if he stayed bitter?

_____

_____

_____

What would be the results of his life if chose to go to the party?

_____

_____

_____

4

PLANNED FEAR

Jeremiah 29:11 - *"For I know the plans I have for you, declares the Lord, plans for welfare and not for evil, to give you a future and a hope."*

God's plan might cause fear.

Why would or could God's plans cause fear? _____
_____
_____
_____

After I had started to heal, they scheduled my first chemo. Doing things for the first time is especially hard for me because I do not like change. Starting chemo with all the scary things I have heard and having no idea what to expect and going to places I have never been was especially scary. In fact, when they gave me my first IV, which has Benadryl in it, they said, "This will make you drowsy." Next thing I knew, I opened my eyes and my friend that had come with me was just sitting there, and it had been two hours. I had been so stressed that when they started with the IV, it knocked me out. I knew that was so, because when I went for rest of my chemo's I was not stressed and in a better frame of mind. The Benadryl just made me feel a little woozy. I never had that reaction again to the IV.

When negative experiences and situations are overwhelming, take a deep breath and focus on things that are true, pure, lovely, and good. Overcoming fear and worry start with controlling our thoughts. I try to keep a positive attitude, but I am also in a spiritual battle. When I am negative, I find that I am sicker and fatigued by the chemo.

I have always been known as a "worry wart."

Do you worry? _____

_____

_____

What do you worry about? _____

_____

_____

Do you know that statistically 40 percent of the things we worry about never happen, 30 percent are in the past and cannot be helped, 12 percent concern the affairs of others that are not our business, 10 percent are about sickness - either real or imagined - and 8 percent are worth worrying about.

I always worried about car accidents and cancer. When I was 17, I broke my back in a head-on car accident and at 55, I was diagnosed with stage 4 Ovarian Cancer. Did my worry stop these? No, it just prevented me from enjoying the day and made me cranky. I still lean towards worrying but it is a lot less, and I have more calmness in my life.

The Webster definition of worry is to feel or show fear and concern because you think that something bad could happen.

What does Psalm 34:4 (***"I sought the Lord, and he answered me and delivered me from all my fears."***) say about fear?

_____

_____

_____

What is fear? _____

_____

_____

According to dictionary.com, fear is a distressing emotion aroused by impending danger, evil, pain, etc., whether the threat is real or imagined; or reverential awe, especially toward God.

The word "fear" occurs 400 times in the Bible.

There is real fear:
When you are out late at night in the dark, real fear makes you cautious.
When we think of death and disease, real fear helps us to live healthily and take certain precautions such as seatbelts, helmets, and sunscreen.
When we read God's Word, fear of God's punishment should encourage us to live Biblically.

We are going to discuss "imagined" fear (worry). This kind of fear prevents us from being all we can be, and that causes us stress. This is the fear that the enemy uses to hinder us and bind us.

We fear.

The enemy has no teeth; but will follow us around testing us to see if we let our guard down, become fearful, and then wants to scare, attack, and kill us.

Isaiah 41:10 says, *"Fear not, for I am with you; be not dismayed, for I am your God; I will strengthen you, I will help you, I will uphold you with my righteous right hand."*

"Fear not" is a command! It is not for a yes and no conversation from us. We have little choice in the matter.

We walk by faith or fear. We have to choose, every single day.

2 Timothy 1:7 says, *"For God gave us a spirit not of fear but of power and love and self-control."*

What does 2 Timothy 1:7 say about fear? _____

_____

_____

Since fear does not come from God, how do you get it?

_____

_____

_____

Hebrew 13:6 adds, *"'The Lord is my helper; I will not fear; what can man do to me?' So that we may boldly say, The Lord is my helper, and I will not fear what man shall do unto me."*

What does Hebrews 13:6 say about fear? _____

_____

_____

There are four ways to help overcome fear. It might be easier to remember using FEAR as an acronym.

1. The F in FEAR is for Faith.

Read John 6:16-21: *"When evening came, his disciples went down to the sea, got into a boat, and started across the sea to Capernaum. It was now dark, and Jesus had not yet come to them. The sea became rough because a strong wind was blowing. When they had rowed about three or four miles, they saw Jesus walking on the sea and coming near the boat, and they were frightened. But he said to them, It is I; do not be afraid."*

Why were they afraid? _____

_____

_____

At the core of it all, they were afraid because they did not expect Jesus to come. They were not ready. They did not trust Him to show up. They thought He was not going to care for them. Maybe they even thought He forgot them. They needed to have faith and look for Jesus to show up. They needed to rest in His promises.

2. The E in FEAR is for Emotional control.

Faith is a mindset that expects Jesus to help!

Read 2 Corinthians 10:5: *"We destroy arguments and every lofty opinion raised against the knowledge of God, and take every thought captive to obey Christ."*

A closer look (using a concordance) is very revealing.

We destroy (Casting down with the use of force; to throw down)
arguments (imaginations or a reasoning; such as is hostile to the Christian faith, men's own purpose and determination of living after their own pleasure)
and every lofty opinion (high thing; "lofty" is not so much "height" as something made high, and belongs to those regions of air where the powers of darkness reside)
raised (exalts itself; exalts themselves against Christ and us)
against the knowledge of God, (true knowledge makes men humble - where there is exaltation of self, the knowledge of God is missing),
and take every thought captive (intent of the mind or will)
to obey Christ (listening to God with resulting action).

Reactions do not come out of the blue. They are a result of the 40,000 thoughts we allow daily. We may not be able to control what comes into our mind, but we do have the power to remove it. Negative thoughts should not be allowed to enter our minds, pull up a seat, and take residence. Remember, 2 Corinthians 10:5 said to destroy those thoughts. Throw them down!

When did or do you let your emotions control your mind?

_____
_____
_____

What was or is the result? _____

_____
_____

How could it have been different? _____

_____
_____

When you think a fearful thought, confess it, and ask God for courage. Then throw it down.

   3. The A in FEAR is for appreciate.

In 2001 the Gallup Poll reported, "The number-one reason most Americans leave their jobs is that they don't feel appreciated. In fact, 65% of people surveyed said they got no recognition for good work last year."

I do not think we are better with God than with each other. We need to express our appreciation more.

Philippians 4:6 says, *"Do not be anxious about anything, but in everything by prayer and supplication with thanksgiving let your requests be made known to God."*

According to this verse, how are we to pray? _____
_____
_____

Is it clear whether this "thanksgiving" is for past blessings or a confidence of what will happen? _____
_____
_____

1 Thessalonians 5:18 says, *"Give thanks in all circumstances; for this is the will of God in Christ Jesus for you."*

People regularly talk about seeking God's will. According to this verse, what is God's will (desire) for us? _____
_____
_____

Develop a habit of focusing on what you are grateful for in the moment. Thank God for his goodness, for your health, for your family and friends, and for the ability to work and create income. Thank him for giving you another day of life and a purpose to fulfill. Thank Him for your problems. The very act of thanking Him releases your mind from its negative focus and in its place. He will give you peace.

List some things you are thankful for:

_____

_____

_____

_____

_____

_____

4. The R in FEAR is for Remember.

We need to remember what God has done.

Deuteronomy 3:21-22 says, *"And I commanded Joshua at that time, 'Your eyes have seen all that the Lord your God has done to these two kings. So will the Lord do to all the kingdoms into which you are crossing. You shall not fear them, for it is the Lord your God who fights for you.'"*

They had already conquered sixty walled cities from Basham. So now, Moses is pointing out, "Look, it is nothing with God. You do not have to worry about the walled cities. You do not have to worry about the giants. If God be for us, who can be against us?" God has promised to go before you and to drive out your enemies. Thus, the things that caused terror and fear in your hearts that destroyed your faith do not need to stop you now, go in. He is seeking to build up their faith in God. Venture out, and let God have an opportunity to work. He is careful to point out that they had already conquered walled cities in the areas of the giants. Joshua had seen it with his own eyes. The more we have seen of the instances of divine wisdom, power, and goodness, the more inexcusable we are if we fear what flesh can do unto us.

What is something God as done for you? _____

_____

_____

_____

God has made an amazing promise.

Deuteronomy 31:6 says, *"Be strong and courageous. Do not fear or be in dread of them, for it is the Lord your God who goes with you. He will not leave you or forsake you."*

What are some of God's promises to you? _____

_____

_____

_____

The Israelites constantly placed items to remind them of what God has done and is going to do. They placed stones at the spot they crossed the Red Sea and the Jordan River. They set containers on their doorpost, hands, and foreheads. Even their diet and clothes had symbolism involved that helped them focus on what God had.

Our culture is constantly using their phone. I set my ringtone to "Our God" by Chris Tomlin. It is a great reminder.

And if our God is for us, then who could ever stop us.
And if our God is with us, then what could stand against.
If God be for us, who can be against us?

What positive reminders have you set in your daily life?

_____

_____

_____

What reminders should you place that would help you have courage daily? _____

_____

_____

FEAR – Faith, Emotional control, Appreciate, Remember

because

FEAR - False Evidence Appearing Real

5

OPERATION IMPACT

J eremiah 29:11 - *"For I know the plans I have for you, declares the Lord, plans for welfare and not for evil, to give you a future and a hope."*

Living life in God's plan impacts others.

1 Timothy 4:12 says, *"Let no one despise you for your youth, but set the believers an example in speech, in conduct, in love, in faith, in purity."*

I have received over 200 cards since my diagnosis; some from people I did not even know knew me. Also, many people have commented on things I had done for/with them in past. Some of the things I do not even remember (of course at this time people do not remember negative things). I have adults that I taught in 5th grade Sunday School follow me on Facebook and state they see me living what I taught them. It is not easy, and I do not always think the way I should, but I try to keep my testimony positive and honoring to GOD. How you live your life will give your words an opportunity to minister and make an impact.

Timothy challenges to set an example in five areas.

1. Speech

How do you (or not) set an example in your speech?

_____

_____

_____

Ephesians 4:29 says, *"Let no corrupting talk come out of your mouths, but only such as is good for building up, as fits the occasion, that it may give grace to those who hear."*

Are you lifting others up or tearing others down with your words?

_____

_____

_____

Are you encouraging others? _____

_____

_____

Can you think of a time when your speech either lifted up or tore down another? _____

_____

_____

Name some traits of speech that are motivated by Satan?

_____

_____

_____

I thought of jealousy, selfishness, earthly concerns and desires, disorder, anger, degrading, and evil.

Pastor Jim says, "You must be little to belittle."

Name some traits of speech that are motivated by God?

_____

_____

_____

I hope that your list included items like the fruit of the Spirit (Galatians 5:22-23) - love, joy, peace, patience, kindness, goodness, faithfulness, gentleness, and self-control. I added mercy, courtesy, yielding to others, sincerity, and being quiet to my list.

2.   Conduct

How do you (or not) set an example in your conduct?

_____

_____

_____

1 Peter 2:12 says, **_"Keep your conduct among the Gentiles honorable, so that when they speak against you as evildoers, they may see your good deeds and glorify God on the day of visitation."_**

Are you conducting yourself in a Christ-like way?

_____

_____

_____

Name some ways that you can conduct yourself that are considered honorable. _____

_____

_____

65

What are things you do that are dishonorable? _____

_____

_____

_____

3.   Love

How do you (or not) set an example in your love? _____

_____

_____

_____

Jesus said in John 13:34, *"A new commandment I give to you, that you love one another: just as I have loved you, you also are to love one another."*

It is a commandment!

Philippians 2:3-4 adds, *"Do nothing from selfish ambition or conceit, but in humility count others more significant than yourselves. Let each of you look not only to his own interests, but also to the interests of others."*

Are you caring for others above yourself? _____

_____

_____

Here are some ways to show love to your neighbor:

• Improve your manners. Be polite to everyone. This includes your husband, your children, your siblings, your parents, the rude cashier, and whomever else God brings along. Be polite even if you do not feel like it.

66

- Take time to be pleasant. Be pleasant to everyone. This includes your husband, your children, your siblings, your parents, the rude cashier, and anyone you come in contact with in stores, church, or anywhere. Do not move so fast that you respond to people curtly. Be pleasant even if you do not feel like it. You will feel better by being pleasant.
- Do not be a "topper." Do not try to "top" everyone else. Your friend says, "You can't believe my morning" and you say, "Oh, I know my morning was horrible." Then you proceed to talk about your morning.
- Do not be a "deflator, spoiler, or downer." Do not "rain on everyone's parade." "I wouldn't go there, the service is horrible," or "That's a dumb place to go on vacation."
- Show interest in other people. This may take time, but it is so worth it. You can do this by commenting in a way to show you are listening and encourage them. "You're right." "I hadn't thought about that." "I see your point." "What do you think?" These statements encourage conversation and make people feel good.
- Smile. If you are a Christian, then you might want to let your face know it.

4. Faith

How do you (or not) set an example in your faith? _____

_____

_____

_____

Matthew 22:37 says, **"And he said to him, "You shall love the Lord your God with all your heart and with all your soul and with all your mind."**

How are you pursuing God first and foremost? _____

_____

_____

_____

Maybe this is an easier way to evaluate your faith. Imagine you were put on trial for being a Christian, what evidence would be brought against you? _____

_____

_____

   5. Purity

How do you (or not) set an example in your purity?

_____

_____

_____

Matthew 5:8 says, **_"Blessed are the pure in heart, for they shall see God."_**

Are you conducting yourself in a pure way? _____

_____

_____

Are you following God's standard of purity or the world's?

_____

_____

_____

What is the difference? _____

_____

_____

1 Timothy 4:12: *"Let no one despise you for your youth, but set the believers an example in speech, in conduct, in love, in faith, in purity."*

Set the example. Be real. Make a difference.

Be a model – role model.

6

TIMING IS EVERYTHING

Jeremiah 29:11 - *"For I know the plans I have for you, declares the Lord, plans for welfare and not for evil, to give you a future and a hope."*

God's plan has perfect timing!

I have spent years scurrying around trying to accomplish things through my own strength and ability. I plan, organize, re-plan, re-organize, and cannot accomplish all I "need." An amazing thing happened when I was so sick. Everything did not fall apart without me doing and scurrying, and I ended up spending quality quiet time with my Lord (we do this when we are in a valley). As I started getting better, I learned that things went smoother when I put God in control of my time. My hope for "us" through this chapter is that we realize when we keep our schedules tentative; God will take care of time.

One day while I was recovering, but at work, a very sweet lady in church sent me flowers with the nicest note (this came on a day that I was very discouraged which shows how God can use people). The bigger blessing was the lady that delivered them paused and Sue, our receptionist, said, "Can I help you?" The lady asked if someone could pray with her. It "just so happens" that Carole, Pastor Jim's wife, was standing right there at that time and prayed with the delivery lady. So it's a good thing this sweet lady listened to the Holy Spirit and sent flowers at the exact right time to encourage me, Sue, the flower delivery person, and Carole.

Do you often say, "I do not have time?" _____
_____
_____

Have you wished for a 30-hour day or an 8-day week? _____
_____
_____

How would a longer day solve our problems? _____
_____
_____
_____

I doubt it would make a lasting difference. We would just fill it with more stuff and wish for more time. It is like having more money; it will not make you less "broke." So many times, we think our problems come from something outside of ourselves. We cannot get the bank account balanced because our spouse does not write down all the withdrawals. We do not finish the Sunday School preparations because the kids will not stay in bed while we try to work on it late at night. Our problem is not that there is not enough time but a problem of priorities.

The greatest danger is letting urgent things crowd out important things.

The issue is that many important tasks seem like they can wait (prayer, Bible study, visiting an elderly friend or parent, serving in ministry, or playing with your child) while we allow "urgent" things (phone calls, Facebook notification, emails, texting, TV shows) demand our time.

What is something that is important that seems to get pushed to the back burner? _____

_____

_____

What are some urgent items that distract you from what is important? What should you do in the future? _____

_____

_____

_____

The truth is that most of our problems stem from allowing the wrong things to have priority.

It takes a special kind of strength to admit that we are our own biggest problem. In the case of the previously mentioned unfinished Sunday School lessons, it may not be completely the kids' fault. If we look at how we spend our time, we will find many gaps. Time is the great equalizer. We all have the same amount of hours in a day and what we choose to do with those hours is up to us. It may feel like it is out of our control, but if we are willing to see it, the truth is that we are choosing. I choose the commitments I made. I choose to watch TV. I choose to throw a shower. I choose to cook homemade meals. I choose to hang out with friends. I choose to teach women. I choose to see my mom. I choose to repaint the kitchen. I choose to take a nap and so on. None of these are bad or wrong. I am not the judge of what should be a priority in your life, but you have enough time. Letting God (through His Spirit) direct you in your activities and commitments (being in God's plan) will bring you enough time and peace.

What "urgent" things are you choosing that keep taking up your time?

_____

_____

_____

What is important to you? _____

_____

_____

What should be important to you that you need to allot more time for? _____

_____

_____

Revelation 2:1-4 says, *"To the angel of the church in Ephesus write: 'The words of him who holds the seven stars in his right hand, who walks among the seven golden lampstands. I know your works, your toil and your patient endurance, and how you cannot bear with those who are evil, but have tested those who call themselves apostles and are not, and found them to be false. I know you are enduring patiently and bearing up for my name's sake, and you have not grown weary. But I have this against you, that you have abandoned the love you had at first.'"*

What did the church of Ephesus abandon, even though they were doing good things? _____

_____

_____

What is this first love? _____

_____

_____

Matthew 22:37-39 has the answer, **"And he said to him, 'You shall love the Lord your God with all your heart and with all your soul and with all your mind. This is the great and first commandment. And a second is like it: You shall love your neighbor as yourself.'"**

This command is repeated in Mark 12:30-31, **"'And you shall love the Lord your God with all your heart and with all your soul and with all your mind and with all your strength.' The second is this: 'You shall love your neighbor as yourself.' There is no other commandment greater than these."**

It has to be understood that something must be important to God for it to even be repeated again: **"And he answered, 'You shall love the Lord your God with all your heart and with all your soul and with all your strength and with all your mind, and your neighbor as yourself'"** (Luke 10:27).

 The Pharisees had come up with some 613 laws. They were meticulous on every detail. Jesus summarized them all with just two: Love God and love your neighbor.

How do we explain love? _____

_____

_____

I once read it this way: "Love can be known only from the actions it prompts. God's love is seen in the gift of His Son."

So how do we love? By action!

Love is a verb. We will give time to whatever and whomever we love. We love what we give time to.

How do you love God? _____
_____
_____

We need to be still and humble and listen to God and not try to figure Him out. B.C. (Before Cancer) I was so busy I did not have time to sit a listen to the Holy Spirit. I quickly did my devotion, quickly prepared my lesson, quickly cleaned my house, and then fit the multiple things I felt I needed to do daily to prove I can do everything. After my surgery, I was forced to sit and even as I felt better, my body refused to do as it did before. While my body was resting, I took time in my devotions, lessons, and praying. I had the opportunity to feel God's peace as I have never before. As Psalm 23:2 says – If I do not take the time to be still, He may make me be still.

Who else are you to Love? _____
_____
_____

Who is your neighbor? _____
_____
_____

Dictionary.com defines "neighbor" as a person or thing that is near another.

Strong's Concordance shows the word in Greek "plesion" which means - any other man (person) irrespective of nation or religion with whom we live by or whom we chance to meet.

How can you love your neighbor? _____
_____
_____

Philippians 2:3-4 adds, *__Do nothing from selfish ambition or conceit, but in humility count others more significant than yourselves. Let each of you look not only to his own interests, but also to the interests of others.__*

So how do we get more time? _____
_____
_____

Four steps to being more productive with your time:

1. Decide what is important. We choose to make our hours count for what we think is important and when we say, "I do not have time" we are saying that person or thing that they/it are not important. It may be I feel more pressure from another task/person or that I enjoy another more but either way, it is a choice I make. I used to say to my mom I would see her more if I had time. What does that say to her?

2. Discover where your time goes. Journal your week to help you figure out what your typical week consists of.

3. Budget your hours. After you do your time chart, see where changes need to be made. Again, remember you make the choices. Letting God (through His Spirit) direct you in your activities and

commitments (being in God's plan) will bring you enough time and peace.

Start small and do not make so many changes at once. Probably these are time habits that have been developed over years, so make slow, steady changes towards how you want your time used.

4. Follow through. Each day evaluate how you want to spend your time. If you cannot say "no" to things, then say, "Let me think it over." Weigh the cost and discern if it is God's will for you. Mark 1:35 shares the secret to Jesus' ministry, *"And rising very early in the morning, while it was still dark, he departed and went out to a desolate place, and there he prayed."*

What is the secret? The key is praying and asking God's direction.

Take out a sheet of paper and write, "Have to, Need to, and Want to" at the top of three columns. Now prioritize your schedule. Work and school are "Have to" level topics. Cutting the grass and vacuuming the house probably fit best under "Need to." Finally, mall shopping, nails, and even hair could fit best with "Want to." (A "Want to" and "Need to" left unattended long enough could become a "Have to.")

How do you rank the following items:

Church –

Prayer –

Devotions –

TV –

Facebook –

Family time –

Time with friends –

Computer time –

Exercise –

7

RELATIONSHIPS

Jeremiah 29:11 - *"For I know the plans I have for you, declares the Lord, plans for welfare and not for evil, to give you a future and a hope."*

Living life in God's plan taught me the importance of relationships.

I really thought I liked being an island. I can handle everything and take care of others. I do not need help. I do care about others, but compassion was not my strong suit. Once you go through a deep valley, you learn a lot about yourself (if you are willing to accept that God has a plan and wants to teach you). You also learn that you need people, and they need you. Before I was challenged by my pride, I would help, but would not take help. Sometimes I need to let others have the blessing of helping. Illness can humble you. It has helped me take a renewed view on relationships.

Below are eight things I learned about relationships.

1. Be you.

God created you in a special way and has a specific plan for your life.

I was always asking people's opinion on if I should do this or that. Even asking people what they thought I should order off a menu or if I should buy certain clothes. This can turn into seeking approval of man instead approval of God. It is dangerous to base your self-worth on whether you are similar to others.

I also "put others first" in a martyr sort of way. I did not want to be selfish and be thinking of myself. Is it actually selfish if you put others first and then you "humbly" tell everyone how you never get what you want or your own way because you are so selfless?

_____

_____

_____

When I was forced to just sit and wonder how long God would allow me to be here, I began to realize it is not selfish to be who God made me to be and to do what the Holy Spirit directed. I did not need to think what would get the most accolades here on earth. What others like to do may not interest you, and what you like to do others may not like. There are talents and gifts you have that others do not. Like we learned in the "Timing is Everything" lesson, if you let the Spirit of God direct you, there is enough time and energy for everything God wants you to do.

Psalm 139:14 brings value and confidence: *"I praise you, for I am fearfully and wonderfully made. Wonderful are your works; my soul knows it very well."*

We are made exactly the way God wanted us to be. We need to like ourselves and not be pressured by others or ourselves to try to be like other people. The devil wants us to feel like we will never measure up to what others think. The opinion we have of ourselves affects our relationships (with God and others), and when we believe Psalm 139:14, we will begin to feel at peace with who we are.

Name something you wish you could do or do better.

_____

_____

_____

Think about why you want that. Maybe you should focus your energies on something that God has given you like a special gift or talent to do.

What special gift or talent do you have? _____

_____

_____

If you were embarrassed to write it down, pause and think, "This is from God, it is a reflection of Him, not me." False humility can be damaging and insulting to God.

How and when should you use this gift or talent? _____

_____

_____

_____

God can and will use us just the way He made us. He will train us and help us overcome areas we are weak in if we are pliable. We do not have to be someone we were not designed by God to be.

Proverbs 23:7 (KJV) says, *"For as he thinketh in his heart, so is he..."*

What does that mean? _____

_____

_____

To be able to accomplish everything God wants in us, we need to speak the positive things God says about us instead of the negative things we "feel."

   2. You reap what you sow.

Galatians 6:7 *"Do not be deceived: God is not mocked, for whatever one sows, that will he also reap."*

If you planted corn in the spring what do you expect to harvest in the summer? _____

_____

_____

If you are snippety, ungracious, and/or impatient with others, what do you expect others to be like towards you? _____

_____

_____

_____

By sowing a better reaction, we will eventually reap better reactions or at the very least reap more peace in our lives. We think that we act because of the way we feel, in fact, we often feel because of the way we act.

Every religion teaches the Silver Rule: Don't do it to others if you don't want it done to you. Only Christianity teaches the Golden Rule: Do unto others as you want done to you.

Christianity is about *"being doers of the Word."*

If you plant to please your own desires (selfishness), you will reap sorrow and stress. If you plant to please God and the Spirit, you will reap joy and peace.

   3. Quit nagging.

Women are known for nagging. It does not mean all women nag, and it definitely does not mean we cannot help it. Nagging is a choice.

Proverbs 27:15-16 *"A continual dripping on a rainy day and a quarrelsome wife are alike; to restrain her is to restrain the wind or to grasp oil in one's right hand."*

Is there someone you tend to nag? _____
_____
_____

Why do you or most women nag? _____
_____
_____

My struggle with nagging tends to be because I like control. I justify it by saying that if I do not stay on top of people things will not get done. Actually, I want it done my way and in my timing. I want to be in control.

   4. Do not "expect" praise or appreciation.

Recognition can be powerful. When someone notices the work I put into something, it goes a long way. However, I should not need the approval of others.

Matthew 6:1-5 says, *"Beware of practicing your righteousness before other people in order to be seen by them, for then you will have no reward from your Father who is in heaven. Thus, when you give to the needy, sound no trumpet before you, as the hypocrites do in the synagogues and in the streets, that they may be praised by others. Truly, I say to you, they have received their reward. But when you give to the needy, do not let your left hand know what your right hand is doing, so that your giving may be in secret. And your Father who sees in secret will reward you. And when you pray, you must not be like the hypocrites. For they love to stand and pray in the synagogues and at the street corners, that they may be seen by others. Truly, I say to you, they have received their reward."*

I love gold stars. Whether or not I should want them, I do. When we are expecting our "gold star" and do not get it, we are discontented and often have a bad attitude with the person we "expected" praise from. Do it for yourself. I "pretend" the things I do, like organizing the cabinets, are for my husband and then I sulk when my husband does not appreciate my efforts. Now, I tell myself, "I'm doing this for myself. This is what I want." This sounds selfish, but in fact, it is less selfish, because it means I am not waiting for a gold star. No one else even has to notice what I have done.

What is something you have done for someone, and did not get any appreciation? _____

_____

Find ways to reward yourself. I give myself my own gold stars by guilt free HGTV watching or allowing myself to get carryout – again, guilt free.

What are some ways you could reward yourself? _____

_____

_____

_____

Tell people you would like to get a gold star. It is easy for people innocently to overlook contributions you have made, and if you give a gentle reminder, they might happily load you with gold stars. I will text Rich and say, "I washed and polished your truck." Now he will know I want to be appreciated. However, he is not a mind reader (he tells me that often) and sometimes he just does not notice.

Express your appreciation for what other people do. One good rule is that if you wish people would act a certain way toward you, act that way yourself toward others. Remember reap what you sow. Remember the Golden Rule. Christianity is active. Do something. Say something. If you wish people would be freer with praise and appreciation, make sure you are being thankful and showing appreciation yourself.

5. Fight right.

Disagreements will come, but we need to be careful what we say and do when we "fight." Obviously, I am not talking about physical combat, as that is never right by man or woman. I am talking about the buttons we push. We need to strive for peace. The disagreement is the enemy, not the other person.

Romans 14:19 *"So then let us pursue what makes for peace and for mutual upbuilding."*

Studies show that letting off steam amplifies, not reduces, anger. I find that the single best technique to avert an argument it to apply humor. If we laugh, the angry mood lifts instantly.

Proverbs 17:22 is just what the doctor ordered, *"A joyful heart is good medicine, but a crushed spirit dries up the bones."*

What are some phrases that lead to peace? _____
_____
_____
_____

Humor is not always the answer. Here are phrases I have needed to say, "Please try to understand my point of view. This is important to me. I overreacted. I had not thought of it that way before. I could be wrong. Let's agree to disagree on that. I am feeling unappreciated. I realize it is not your fault. That came out all wrong. What are we really fighting about? How can I make things better? I am sorry. I love you."

6. No grumbling.

When people grumble, it drains me. It can suck the life out of me. Therefore, when I grumble, it must do the same to others.

Philippians 2:14 *"Do all things without grumbling or disputing."*

Complaining to others opens the door for sins such as self-pity and anger. This leads to bitterness, which leads to malice. Whenever you need to complain or grumble, go to God. He understands better than anybody the stresses and strains that have afflicted you. When you vent to Him, He can temper your thoughts and help you see things from His perspective. He will then put His thoughts in your mind and a song in your heart.

People do not want to hear us whining about our troubles.

Is there something you tend to whine about? _____

_____
_____
_____

Is there someone you continually unload on? _____

_____
_____
_____

As the old adage goes, "Be a winner, not a whiner."

   7. Show proofs of love.

Love is often defined as a feeling. It is a feeling or affection, but it does not stop there. Love changes us. It causes us to do things we generally would not. It is more than just a feeling; it is an action. Love does.

John 14:23 says, ***"Jesus answered him, "If anyone loves me, he will keep my word, and my Father will love him, and we will come to him and make our home with him."***

There is no love without proofs of love (love is a verb which means it is an action). This verse is how we prove our love to Jesus.

How do you prove your love to your husband, children, friends, and others? _____

_____

_____

Good relationships do not "just happen." We need to express our love by things we do, not just what we say. "Actions speak louder than words," is a true statement.

Studies show we will feel 47% closer to those who we express affection to.

What are some ways you can show love? _____

_____

_____

   8. Be forgiving.

"And you know, when you've experienced grace and you feel like you've been forgiven, you're a lot more forgiving of other people. You're a lot more gracious to others." Rick Warren

Since we have been forgiven, we should also forgive.

Proverbs 20:22 says, ***"Do not say, 'I will repay evil'; wait for the Lord, and he will deliver you."***

Let God be God.

Proverbs 24:29 ***"Do not say, 'I will do to him as he has done to me; I will pay the man back for what he has done.'"***

Paybacks never end. It becomes a cycle of one-upping each other.

Proverbs 19:11 *"Good sense makes one slow to anger, and it is his glory to overlook an offense."*

Sometimes it is just better to be wronged and move on. God knows.

Ephesians 4:31-32 *"Let all bitterness and wrath and anger and clamor and slander be put away from you, along with all malice. Be kind to one another, tenderhearted, forgiving one another, as God in Christ forgave you."*

The dictionary definition of forgive is to cease to feel resentment against an offender, i.e., to pardon one's enemies.

What kind of offense do you find most difficult to forgive?

_____

_____

_____

Do you meditate on an offense repeatedly? _____

_____

_____

How do you find it in yourself to let go of past offenses?

_____

_____

_____

Does forgiving someone mean that the offense is forgotten?

_____

_____

_____

A great image of forgiveness is that of a paper shredder. An offense against us is like an IOU, and we put that IOU right through the shredder. It is not forgotten, but it cannot be used against the person in the future.

There is only one phrase in the Lord's Prayer with a "condition" attached:

"And forgive us our debts, as we also have forgiven our debtors" (Matthew 6:12). Be careful how you pray. Are you able to ask God to forgive you in the same manner that you forgive others? _____

_____
_____
_____

These are the eight things I learned about relationships:

1. Be you.
2. You reap what you sow.
3. Quit nagging.
4. Do not "expect" praise or appreciation.
5. Fight right.
6. No grumbling.
7. Show proofs of love.
8. Be forgiving.

What item will you work on today? _____

_____
_____
_____

PURPOSE

J eremiah 29:11 - *"For I know the plans I have for you, declares the Lord, plans for welfare and not for evil, to give you a future and a hope."*

Living life in God's plan gives us purpose.

At the beginning of 2014, I was the legal treasurer of the church and in charge of all finances and was still the "senior" pastor's administrative assistant. By September, I was "just" the office manager and mostly doing data entry. I was just entering attendance and setting systems to track people. By the world's standard, I had been demoted. By God's standards, He had a different (but just as important) job for me. We cannot be upset if we do not have a place of prominence. God gives special honor to people with "less honorable" roles.

Are there any responsibilities, chores, or a job that you feel are beneath you?_____

_____

_____

Where would you rather get "your honor" from, man or God?

_____

_____

_____

1 Corinthians 12:21-24 says, *"The eye cannot say to the hand, 'I have no need of you,' nor again the head to the feet, 'I have no need of you.' On the contrary, the parts of the body that seem to be weaker are indispensable, and on those parts of the body that we think less honorable we bestow the greater honor, and our unpresentable parts are treated with greater modesty, which our more presentable parts do not require. But God has so composed the body, giving greater honor to the part that lacked it."*

When I took a gift test years ago, my gift was "leadership." Meaning I can or like to "boss" people around and expect them to act how I want. It is my gift.

When I took the gift test recently, it said, "Your gift is to serve and render assistance to others with compassion and grace. You have a broad range of possibilities to apply your service and bring forth impact. You have a unique ability to identify areas that need help and those who are struggling. You have an understanding and compassionate demeanor that is crucial to the edification." I do not think of myself this way, but God must have. Actually, leadership and service should go together.

How do leadership and serving work together?_____

_____

_____

_____

I mentioned to Pastor Jim about my struggles with the changes and he said, "With these changes and your journey, God can use you so much more in Ladies' Ministry." This is a place I never saw myself years ago, but God had the "perfect" plan, and I love serving the ladies.

We need to serve God daily in whatever capacity He wants us, and He may change us for His use.

We cannot compare ourselves to others or give up if someone else "does it better." There will always be those who have more talent.

How would the Gospel be spread if evangelists, teachers, or yourself, gave up because someone did a better job?

_____

_____

_____

Where is an area God is nudging you to get involved?

_____

_____

_____

Knowing God has a perfect plan for our life, I think there are three conditions needed in finding God's will for our life.

1. BE PREPARED

People want to know God's plan for their lives, yet all too often, they sit around hoping it will mysteriously be revealed to them.

How can you find your purpose? _____

_____

_____

_____

1 Thessalonians 4:4 (KJV): *"That every one of you should know how to possess his vessel in sanctification and honour."*

2 Timothy 2:21(KJV): *"If a man therefore purge himself from these, he shall be a vessel unto honour, sanctified, and meet for the master's use, and prepared unto every good work."*

The generic meaning of sanctification is "the state of proper functioning." To sanctify someone or something is to set that person or thing apart for the use intended by its designer. A pen is "sanctified" when used to write. Eyeglasses are "sanctified" when used to improve sight. In the theological sense, things are sanctified when they are used for the purpose God intends. A human being is sanctified, therefore, when he or she lives according to God's design and purpose.

Our church has a daily devotion that is available on our app, website, or can be emailed each day. Phil, one of our music directors recently wrote, "Sanctification is the incredible process that a person goes through as he or she develops in their spiritual life."

True sanctification begins with renewing your mind. You must know the truth, plain and simple. You are not going to get there by osmosis. Growth requires the discipline of constantly putting God's truth in your mind. Apart from the Scripture, there is no way to restrain your sinful flesh.

As you learn God's truth, it will produce principles that you do not desire to violate. That is sanctification. It is the transformation of your heart and your will that compels you to obey God's Word.

Discuss: Why do you need to be "prepared" to have purpose for God? _____

_____

_____

_____

What do you need to work on right now?_____

_____

_____

_____

We need to be prepared so that in God's perfect timing we are ready and able to accomplish much for Him as He works through us.

2. BE STILL

We tend to be constantly on the go. It seems there is always something to do and somewhere to go. It is difficult to just stop. We need to hit the pause button on our life and "be still."

Psalm 46:10 says, ***"Be still, and know that I am God. I will be exalted among the nations, I will be exalted in the earth!"***

Be still in Hebrew is "raphah." It means to let drop, abandon, relax, refrain, let go, let alone, and be quiet. This seems relatively simple, but it is tough. Without being intentional, we easily get caught up in "the captivity of activity." We may be busy doing things that are of God or are good, but we need to be still to really know God. This is when we feel His presence, His peace, and His strength.

How can you "be still" this week? _____

_____
_____
_____

Is there a specific time or place that makes "being still" easier?

_____
_____
_____

Find some time alone. Eliminate all sound, get comfortable, and just think about God. Think about who He is and what He has done. See how long it is before your mind wanders. Is it 10 minutes, 5 minutes, or just 2 minutes? It is during this time when you will hear His voice, and He will guide you in what is His purpose for you. As we have learned, peace comes from being in His plan.

By silencing our hearts, we can absorb His will.

3. BE WILLING

Is it possible to pray too much? _____

_____
_____
_____

I think people pray for opportunities. They are ready and able, but not necessarily willing. They want to pray about it some more. People resist commitments. If God has made it clear on what needs to be done, stop praying and start doing (obviously you can and should pray continually while you are acting upon the opportunity).

Romans 12:4-8 *"For as in one body we have many members, and the members do not all have the same function, so we, though many, are one body in Christ, and individually members one of another. Having gifts that differ according to the grace given to us, let us use them: if prophecy, in proportion to our faith; if service, in our serving; the one who teaches, in his teaching; the one who exhorts, in his exhortation; the one who contributes, in generosity; the one who leads, with zeal; the one who does acts of mercy, with cheerfulness."*

Moses is a good example of a man that was prepared and spent time with God and was willing, so he knew his purpose, but he had some of the same struggles we have. Even Moses said, "Here am I, send Aaron."

What hinders us from being willing?_____
_____
_____
_____

Read Exodus 2:11-12 *"One day, when Moses had grown up, he went out to his people and looked on their burdens, and he saw an Egyptian beating a Hebrew, one of his people. He looked this way and that, and seeing no one, he struck down the Egyptian and hid him in the sand."*

What hindered Moses? _____

_____

_____

_____

Chuck Smith's commentary states: Now some say the mistake was "he looked this way and that way," but he didn't look up. We make that mistake so often. We look this way and that way, and then we act, not realizing that God sees us. He tried to hide his deed by burying the Egyptian in the sand.

Moses had a sense of destiny. Perhaps because of his position, he felt that he was destined to lead these people out of their bondage. He seemed to have this awareness and consciousness. He was surprised that they did not recognize it. The problem with Moses was that he just got ahead of God. He tried to do what God wanted done in the ability and in the power of his own flesh. Knowing what God wanted, aware of the purposes of God, his big mistake was getting ahead of God. We often make this mistake. We know what God wants to do, but we do not wait for God or His empowering to do it. We try to do in the energy of our own flesh.

Moses got ahead of God. He overreacted.

Read Exodus 3:10-11: *"'Come, I will send you to Pharaoh that you may bring my people, the children of Israel, out of Egypt.' But Moses said to God, 'Who am I that I should go to Pharaoh and bring the children of Israel out of Egypt?'"*

Exodus 4:10-13 also gives Moses perspective, *"But Moses said to the Lord, 'Oh, my Lord, I am not eloquent, either in the past or since you have spoken to your servant, but I am slow of speech and of tongue.' Then the Lord said to him, 'Who has made man's mouth? Who makes him mute, or deaf, or*

seeing, or blind? Is it not I, the Lord? Now therefore go,
and I will be with your mouth and teach you what you shall
speak.' But he said, 'Oh, my Lord, please send someone
else.'"

What hindered Moses from fulfilling his purpose? _____

_____

_____

_____

We are good at making excuses. It is shameful that we doubt God.

Have you told God "no" to His purpose because you did not believe
He could empower you? _____

_____

_____

_____

Acts 7:22 gives a different perspective or description on Moses,
"And Moses was instructed in all the wisdom of the
Egyptians, and he was mighty in his words and deeds."

Do you think Moses was a gifted speaker and denied it or that he did
struggle with words but God blessed his efforts? _____

_____

_____

_____

_____

When God calls - JUST DO IT!

Be prepared.

Be still.

Be willing.

And then step out of the boat.

9

TRUTHFUL THOUGHTS

J eremiah 29:11 - *"For I know the plans I have for you, declares the Lord, plans for welfare and not for evil, to give you a future and a hope."*

Living life in God's plan is based on facts.

I ran into an old friend, and she could not believe how good I looked for having cancer and six months of chemo. I have had people say this to me even without hair, eyelashes, or eyebrows. I did ponder what people might be seeing because it is not a "physical" good look. God laid the following verse on my heart.

Isaiah 26:3 *"You keep him in perfect peace whose mind is stayed on you, because he trusts in you."*

On 11/16/2015 as I am proofing this lesson to prepare for next week, I have just been at my six-month checkup. My CT scan shows multiple masses, which indicates recurrence of Ovarian Cancer. I (against my doctor's instruction) looked this up online, and it is scary. However, God had chosen this lesson to be reviewed this week. Isn't he awesome!

We have to keep our mind on Him. Focus on the facts.

Matthew 14:25-33 *"And in the fourth watch of the night he came to them, walking on the sea. But when the disciples saw him walking on the sea, they were terrified, and said, 'It is a ghost!' and they cried out in fear. But immediately Jesus spoke to them, saying, 'Take heart; it is I. Do not be afraid.' And Peter answered him, 'Lord, if it is you, command me to come to you on the water.' He said, 'Come.' So Peter got out of the boat and walked on the water and came to Jesus. But when he saw the wind, he was afraid, and beginning to sink he cried out, 'Lord, save me.' Jesus immediately reached out his hand and took hold of him, saying to him, 'O you of little faith, why did you doubt?' And when they got into the boat, the wind ceased. And those in the boat worshiped him, saying, 'Truly you are the Son of God.'"*

Peter knew it was the Lord, but he still said, "If."

How many times do you hear yourself saying, "If"?

_____

_____

_____

"But when" speaks of life. As soon as the trials of life blow in, we doubt.

What is your "but when" that makes you afraid?

_____

_____

_____

Jesus asks, "Why did you doubt?"

Your feelings will lie to you, and you will sink like a rock in the sea.

Jeremiah 17:9 says, *"The heart is deceitful above all things, and desperately sick; who can understand it?"*

Do not let your feelings (based perception of the situation) guide your actions.

Focus on the facts.

Where do we find the facts? We find them in the Word of God.

Please read the following verses:

Philippians 4:8: *"Finally, brothers, whatever is true, whatever is honorable, whatever is just, whatever is pure, whatever is lovely, whatever is commendable, if there is any excellence, if there is anything worthy of praise, think about these things."*

What do you think on? _____
_____
_____
_____

What should you think on? _____
_____
_____
_____

Colossians 3:1-2: *"If then you have been raised with Christ, seek the things that are above, where Christ is, seated at the right hand of God. Set your minds on things that are above, not on things that are on earth."*

What should you set your mind on?_____

_____

_____

_____

Mark 8:33: *"But turning and seeing his disciples, he rebuked Peter and said, 'Get behind me, Satan! For you are not setting your mind on the things of God, but on the things of man.'"*

Who messes with your mind? _____

_____

_____

_____

The Firebird story: What if God's love were like the sun, constant and unchanging? What if one day you realized nothing could take that away?

Firebird is a bright orange baby Oriole, who just loves the sunshine. However, whenever a storm blows in, he frets and asks Mama why God allows the rain to take the sun away. When Firebird is finally old enough, his mother gently instructs him to fly up through the thunder and lightning to see what is on the other side.

It is a rough flight, and just when he is about to give up, Firebird rises above the storm to discover the sun shining where it always had been.

God never lets the storm take the sun away. With that truth in his heart, Firebird continues to bask in the sunshine, but just as important, he learns to rejoice in the rain.

Why do you think Firebird complained during the storm?

_____

_____

_____

When do you complain? _____

_____

_____

_____

Tell about a time you trusted your feelings.

_____

_____

_____

What should you trust in? _____

_____

_____

_____

Think about what you are thinking about.

Think truthful thoughts.

10

CONTENTMENT

Jeremiah 29:11 - *"For I know the plans I have for you, declares the Lord, plans for welfare and not for evil, to give you a future and a hope."*

Living life in God's plan provides contentment. Material things do not satisfy.

What are some things you want in life? _____

_____

_____

_____

What are some things you think God wants for you in life?

_____

_____

_____

Ecclesiastes 6:9 says, *"Better is the sight of the eyes than the wandering of the appetite: this also is vanity and a striving after wind."*

1 Timothy 6:6-10 adds, *"But godliness with contentment is great gain, for we brought nothing into the world, and we cannot take anything out of the world. But if we have food and clothing, with these we will be content. But those who desire to be rich fall into temptation, into a snare, into many senseless and harmful desires that plunge people into ruin and destruction. For the love of money is a root of all kinds of evils. It is through this craving that some have wandered away from the faith and pierced themselves with many pangs."*

What is godliness? _____
_____
_____
_____

What is contentment? _____
_____
_____

What happens to a person whose sole desire is to be rich?
_____
_____
_____

The world's way of pursuing riches is grasping and hoarding. You attain His riches by letting go and giving.

The Bible says the love of money is the root of all kinds of evil. We can see the effects of materialism in the world, and the more we have, the more dissatisfied we are. We have lots.

What is the number one growing business in the United States?

It is storage units. We have so much "good stuff" that we cannot contain it all. Some day we may need it. You should see the size of the closets in my 1957 house. Times have changed. We have become materialistic.

Do you struggle with wanting more? _____

_____

_____

Studies show that 87% of all people that won the lottery or came into an inheritance eventually end up bankrupt, depressed, divorced...unhappy. The rush of happiness will usually cause you to spend more than you can afford and that leads to remorse.

Do you have a possession or hobby that is financially getting out of control? _____

_____

_____

Proverbs 15:17 says, *"Better is a dinner of herbs where love is than a fattened ox and hatred with it."*

Would you prefer to sit down at a table where there is only bread and water but a wonderful atmosphere of love or to a table loaded with goodies where everyone growls at each other?

_____

_____

_____

Read Hebrews 13:5 *"Keep your life free from love of money, and be content with what you have, for he has said, 'I will never leave you nor forsake you.'"*

Money often stands for things we feel we are lacking.

What would you do with a sudden burst of money (10,000 or even 100,000)? _____

_____

_____

We need to stay off the hedonic (pleasure seeking) treadmill (Wikipedia describes hedonic treadmill as when a person makes more money, expectations and desires rise in tandem, which results in no permanent gain in happiness). The more of something we have, the less happy it makes us which causes us to desire more because what we already have we think we "need." People in India appreciate fresh water; we think we "need" cable.

What do you need? _____

_____

_____

There are three things the world offers that encompasses all sin.

1 John 2:16 says, *"For all that is in the world—the desires of the flesh and the desires of the eyes and pride of life—is not from the Father but is from the world."*

1 John 2:16 (NLT) clarifies, *"For the world offers only a craving for physical pleasure, a craving for everything we see, and pride in our achievements and possessions. These are not from the Father, but are from this world."*

When we allow one or all of these in our life, the enemy will have victory.

Being in God's Word, listening to His Word, and studying His word is the key way to overcome the world.

It is interesting to see how **the desires of the flesh and the desires of the eyes and pride of life** play out in two familiar Bible stories.

1. Eve (and Adam)

They believed the lie and did not consult the Word of God.

Genesis 3:1-6 *"Now the serpent was more crafty than any other beast of the field that the Lord God had made. He said to the woman, 'Did God actually say, 'You shall not eat of any tree in the garden?' And the woman said to the serpent, 'We may eat of the fruit of the trees in the garden, but God said, 'You shall not eat of the fruit of the tree that is in the midst of the garden, neither shall you touch it, lest you die.' But the serpent said to the woman, 'You will not surely die. For God knows that when you eat of it your eyes will be opened, and you will be like God, knowing good and evil.' So when the woman saw that the tree was good for food, and that it was a delight to the eyes, and that the tree was to be desired to make one wise, she took of its fruit and ate, and she also gave some to her husband who was with her, and he ate."*

Satan causes us to doubt by twisting God's Word. He then uses his three tricks:

So when the woman saw that the tree was good for food, (lust of the flesh - craving for physical desires and that which is forbidden).

117

and that it was a delight to the eyes (lust of the eyes – wanting what we see but don't have).

and that the tree was to be desired to make one wise, (pride of life – trusting in our own power and resources).

What was the result of Adam and Eve's choices?

_____

_____

_____

We need to remember our choices affect others.

    2. Christ

He did not believe the lie and used the Word of God.

Matthew 4:1-11 ***"Then Jesus was led up by the Spirit into the wilderness to be tempted by the devil. And after fasting forty days and forty nights, he was hungry. And the tempter came and said to him, 'If you are the Son of God, command these stones to become loaves of bread.' But he answered, 'It is written, Man shall not live by bread alone, but by every word that comes from the mouth of God.' Then the devil took him to the holy city and set him on the pinnacle of the temple and said to him, 'If you are the Son of God, throw yourself down, for it is written, 'He will command his angels concerning you,' And 'On their hands they will bear you up, lest you strike your foot against a stone.' Jesus said to him, 'Again it is written, 'You shall not put the Lord your God to the test.' Again, the devil took him to a very high mountain and showed him all the kingdoms of the world and their glory. And he said to him, 'All these I will*** *give you, if you will fall down and worship me.' Then Jesus said to him, 'Be gone, Satan! For it is written, You shall worship the Lord your God and him only shall you serve.' Then the devil left him, and behold, angels came and were ministering to him."*

Then Jesus was led up by the Spirit into the wilderness to be tempted by the devil. After fasting forty days and forty nights, he was hungry. Then the tempter came. He usually comes when we are weary, wounded, and wandering. He challenged Him with all three weapons.

"Stones to become loaves of bread" uses the lust of the flesh – tempting him when physically hungry.

"He will command his angels concerning you" injects the pride of life – trust in what the world or I can do.

"All these I will give you" is an attempt to use the lust of the eyes – tempting us with things we see and might desire that are not God's will for our life.

I judge my relationship with the Lord by where I rate in these areas:

Physically (lust of the flesh) - Am I preoccupied with something that feels good? Am I trying to satisfy physical desires over demonstrating control? _____

_____

_____

Emotionally (lust of the eye) – Am I always seeing things I want or that look good? Am I preoccupied with accumulating things over demonstrating generosity? _____

_____

_____

Psychologically (pride of life) – Do I regularly want something to impress others? Am I preoccupied with boasting of what one has and does over demonstrating humble service? _____

_____

_____

_____

In what areas of life do you struggle with these?

Lust of the eyes –

Lust of the flesh –

Pride of life –

What bible verse should you memorize relating to these?

Lust of the eyes –

Lust of the flesh –

Pride of life –

Use your Bible. It has been said, "Clean Bible, dirty heart. Dirty Bible, clean heart." We need to be in the Word daily preparing for the darts of the enemy.

"For the word of God is living and active, sharper than any two-edged sword, piercing to the division of soul and of spirit, of joints and of marrow, and discerning the thoughts and intentions of the heart" (Hebrews 4:12).

11

GOD IS GOOD

J eremiah 29:11 - *"For I know the plans I have for you, declares the Lord, plans for welfare and not for evil, to give you a future and a hope."*

God's plan is always good.

God is good all the time and all the time God is good!

Psalm 145:1-3 *"I will extol you, my God and King, and bless your name forever and ever. Every day I will bless you and praise your name forever and ever. Great is the Lord, and greatly to be praised, and his greatness is unsearchable."*

While my husband and I were in oncologist's office, the doctor read my CT scan report and said he thought it looked to him like it was just a benign ovarian cyst, but there was a 9% chance it was cancer. I remember texting my kids and they were so happy. They were all praising God.

After my surgery and they had thought it was stage 4 Appendiceal Cancer (less than 12% survival for 2 years), was God still good?

Then we find out it is actually Stage 3 Ovarian Cancer, better chances but still…. Is God still good?

Now it has been over a year since my diagnosis and at my six-month checkup and CT scan, we were told I have multiple masses and a CA125 number of 183, which confirms a recurrence of Ovarian Cancer. Is God still good?

From Rabbi Kushner's book "When Bad Things Happen to Good People," he reaches a disturbing conclusion. He suggests that we are forced to choose between a good God, who is not totally powerful or a powerful God who is not totally good. If God cares He is not strong, if He is strong He does not care.

However, according to the Bible God is strong and He cares.
God is strong!

2 Samuel 22:33 says, *"This God is my strong refuge and has made my way blameless."*

God cares!

1 Peter 5:7 says, *"Casting all your anxieties on him, because he cares for you."*

So what is the problem? _____
_____
_____

What is your priority? _____
_____
_____

What is God's priority? _____

_____

_____

The problem is our human agenda. We want good health, good income, and a good night's rest.

Our priority is "we." God's priority is God.

Isaiah 48:10-11 shows God's priority, ***"Behold, I have refined you, but not as silver; I have tried you in the furnace of affliction. For my own sake, for my own sake, I do it, for how should my name be profaned? My glory I will not give to another."***

"He does not ask how can I make you happy, but how can I use you to display my excellence? He may use blessings or buffetings, but both belong to Him" (excerpts from Mac Lucado's book "Come Thirsty").

From my Sarah Young, "Jesus Calling" devotional: "People tend to think circumstances determine the quality of their lives. So they put their energy into trying to control those situations. They feel happy when things are going well and sad or frustrated when things don't go as they hoped or expected. They rarely question this correlation between circumstances and feelings. It is possible to be content in any and every situation. Put more energy into trusting Him and enjoying His presence."

Endure for Eternity – Excerpt from our church devotional written by Noble, Director of Guest Services:

"Life is tough. If it were easy, there would be no such things as depression, suicide, hurt, anger, fear, sadness, doubt, and hate. But life is tough. As followers of Christ, we are going to face many trials and have to deal with things we hate, so that He can be glorified through us. James writes about this in James 1:2-3, *"Count it all joy, my brothers, when you meet trials of various kinds, for you know that the testing of your faith produces steadfastness."* So, when those hardships and things we hate come into our lives, endure. Endure and remember that through those trials, you are being used for His glory."

Are there areas of your life that you think God cannot handle?

_____

_____

_____

Are there times in your life when you feel God does not care?

_____

_____

_____

How are you going to change your perspective?_____

_____

_____

_____

God is good all the time and all the time God is good.

12

LIVING FOR CHRIST

One of the most common verses at funerals is Philippians 1:21: *"For to me to live is Christ, and to die is gain."*

When you look at the verse are you immediately comforted by the phrase *"and to die is gain?"* _____
_____
_____

Dee chose to focus on the first seven words, "For to me to live is Christ." She focused on living every day for Christ.

She chose to keep her Facebook ministry active until her last two weeks on earth. Be challenged. Choose to live for Christ. By the way, you will get Heaven.

DeeAnn Robinson Moshier at ♥ St. Joseph Mercy
Oakland Hospital
February 7 • Pontiac

Are you God-focused or giant-focused?

👍 Like 💬 Comment ↗ Share

DeeAnn Robinson Moshier at ♥ St. Joseph Mercy
Oakland Hospital
February 7 • Pontiac

God has blessed me with more "good days"
through this journey than "bad days"
This picture was only 4 months after surgery
while in chemo and I could still enjoy a fun day
with my Dean.

👍 Like 💬 Comment ↗ Share

DeeAnn Robinson Moshier at ♥ St. Joseph Mercy
Oakland Hospital
February 7 • Pontiac

I Samuel 17:37 And David said, "The Lord who
delivered me from the paw of the lion and from
the paw of the bear will deliver me from the
hand of this Philistine."

He will deliver you from your giant.

👍 Like 💬 Comment ↗ Share

130

DeeAnn Robinson Moshier at 📍 St. Joseph Mercy
Oakland Hospital
March 16 • Pontiac

For those that are curious – I had my 3rd CT
scan. I am sad to report that this recurrence of
cancer is NOT responding to chemo.

👍 Like   💬 Comment   ↗ Share

DeeAnn Robinson Moshier at 📍 St. Joseph Mercy
Oakland Hospital
March 16 • Pontiac

I am blessed to report: I have a GOD who loves
me and is GOOD and has a plan for my life.
Jeremiah 29:11
"For I know the plans I have for you, declares
the Lord, plans for good and not for evil, to
give you a future and a hope."

👍 Like   💬 Comment   ↗ Share

DeeAnn Robinson Moshier at 📍 St. Joseph Mercy
Oakland Hospital
April 16 • Pontiac

This has been the most challenging month of
my life. Through it all I have seen God in small
and large ways when I SEEK HIM, His strength
and His presence. (Psalm 105:4)

👍 Like   💬 Comment   ↗ Share

DeeAnn Robinson Moshier at ♥ St. Joseph Mercy Oakland Hospital
April 23 • Pontiac

Trusting God that HE knows the perfect plan and timing for my healing. Could also still use prayers. Jeremiah 29:11

👍 Like   💬 Comment   ➤ Share

DeeAnn Robinson Moshier at ♥ St. Joseph Mercy Oakland Hospital
April 24 • Pontiac

It has been since Good Friday that I have been home. Please pray I continue to be strong and trust and honor God. I do know HIS plan is perfect.

👍 Like   💬 Comment   ➤ Share

DeeAnn Robinson Moshier at ♥ St. Joseph Mercy Oakland Hospital
May 10 • Pontiac

God is so good to me supplying life and a home to go to, an awesome husband, loving children and such a supportive group of family and friends. Please pray for continued healing.

👍 Like   💬 Comment   ➤ Share

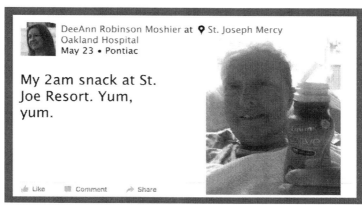

DeeAnn Robinson Moshier at ♥ St. Joseph Mercy Oakland Hospital
May 23 • Pontiac

My 2am snack at St. Joe Resort. Yum, yum.

Like   Comment   Share

DeeAnn Robinson Moshier at ♥ St. Joseph Mercy Oakland Hospital
May 23 • Pontiac

I am not sure why this is my journey but I do KNOW God is good all the time and all the time God is good. Jeremiah 29:11

Like   Comment   Share

DeeAnn Robinson Moshier at ♥ St. Joseph Mercy Oakland Hospital
May 23 • Pontiac

IF your law had not been my delight, I would have perished in my affliction.
Psalm 119:92 and HIS law is my delight and I will flourish in this affliction.

Like   Comment   Share

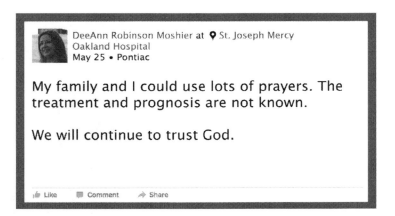

DeeAnn Robinson Moshier at ♀ St. Joseph Mercy Oakland Hospital
May 25 • Pontiac

My family and I could use lots of prayers. The treatment and prognosis are not known.

We will continue to trust God.

👍 Like   💬 Comment   ➤ Share

the beginning...

Made in the USA
Charleston, SC
29 August 2016